Coloring Books Ages 9-12

Copyright © 2016 Violet Brown

All rights reserved. No part of this book may be reproduced or transmitted in any form or by any means, including but not limited to information storage and retrieval systems,electronic,mechanical,photocopy,recording,etc. without written permission from the copyright holder.

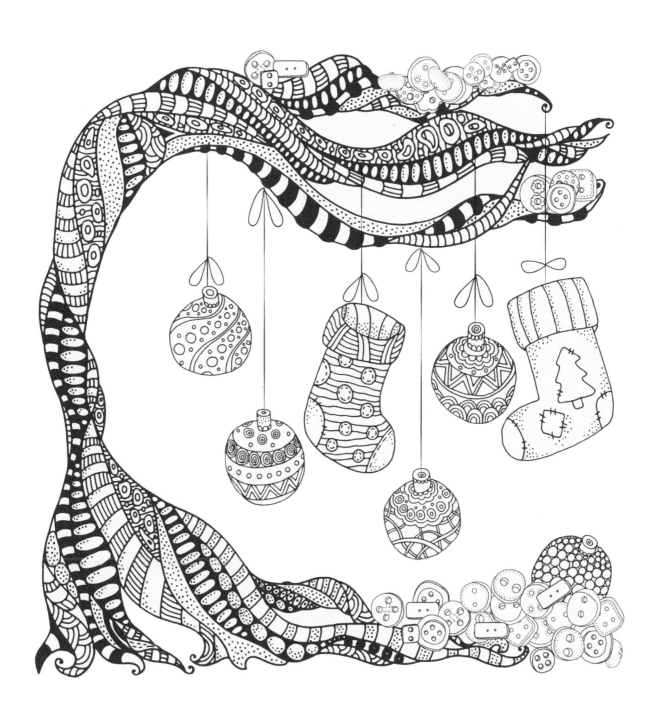

Thank you so much again for buying this book! I hope you enjoyed coloring my book. Now I'd like ask for a *small* favor. Could you please take a minute or two and leave a review for this book Amazon. It'd be greatly appreciated! And I truly value your opinion and thoughts and I will incorporate them into my next book, which is already underway.

CPSIA information can be obtained
at www.ICGtesting.com
Printed in the USA
LVHW102131260320
651347LV00006B/157